For my own special family

Photographs by Andre Martin
Costumes designed by Katrina Melatopolou
Design and art direction by Debbie MacKinnon
Thank you to all the lovely children who acted out the story:
Alena, Amelia, Anja, Avalon, Chloe, Elliot, Fabian, James, Lyndon, Marlon, Nayibe,
Patrick, Scott, Timothy, Thomas, Verity

This edition published by Concordia Publishing House
3558 S. Jefferson Avenue, St. Louis, MO 63118-3968
Away in a Manger copyright Frances Lincoln Limited 2000
Text copyright © 2000 Debbie MacKinnon
Photographs copyright © 2000 Debbie MacKinnon
First published in Great Britain in 2000 by
Frances Lincoln Limited
4 Torriano Mews, Torriano Avenue,
London NW5 2RZ

ISBN 0-570-07114-3
Printed in Hong Kong

1   2   3   4   5   6   7   8   9   10   09 08 07 06 05 04 03 02 01 00

Away in a Manger

The Christmas Story
retold by Debbie MacKinnon
Photographs by Andre Martin

CPH
Concordia Publishing House

Alena, Marlon, and Patrick are very excited. So are Tom and Amelia, Fabian, Elliot, Nayibe and Anja. No one can keep still, everyone is jumping around and chattering.

"Where's my halo?"

"I've lost the frankincense, but here are the crooks..."

"Where shall we put the manger?"

"Keep still Nayibe, while I fix your wings!"

"Hold on to that lamb, Tom!"

The children are getting ready to tell you the wonderful story of Christmas.

"Now, are you all ready?
The story is about to begin..."

Long, long ago, a young woman named Mary lived in the village of Nazareth. She was about to marry Joseph, a kind man who worked as a carpenter.

One day, as Mary was busy around the house, an angel appeared before her. The angel had come with a very special message. "Do not be afraid, Mary," said the angel. "God is sending you a son and His name shall be Jesus."

Mary was very happy and excited that God had chosen her to be the mother of His Son.

Soon Mary and Joseph were married, but before the baby was born, they had to leave their house in Nazareth and travel far away to Bethlehem, where Joseph's family had come from. The Roman emperor had ordered that everyone must return to the birthplace of their family to be counted and pay their taxes.

It was a long and tiring journey. When they finally arrived, Bethlehem was packed with crowds of people. There was no room for Mary and Joseph to stay at the inn.

Mary knew it was nearly time for her baby to be born and she felt very weary.

"You can stay in the stable with the animals," said the innkeeper. "At least you will be warm and dry in there."

Mary was glad to rest at last.

That night Mary's baby was born in the stable.

"Welcome, Jesus," She whispered as she gently laid the baby in a manger to sleep.

Nearby, some shepherds were watching their sheep in the fields. Suddenly a dazzling angel appeared out of the darkness and all the shepherds were terrified. "Fear not," said the angel. "I bring you good tidings of great joy."

Today a baby has been born in Bethlehem and He will be your Savior, Christ the Lord. You will find the baby lying in a manger." At once, the sky was full of light and angels singing, "Glory to God in the highest, and on earth peace, goodwill toward men."

In an instant, the angels were gone, the sky was dark again, and the shepherds were alone.

"We must go and find the baby," the shepherds said to each other. So they hurried to Bethlehem. They found Jesus in the stable with Mary and Joseph, just as the angel had told them.

The shepherds knelt down to look at the sleeping child, saying, "Praise the Lord!"

Then they quietly slipped away to tell the wonderful news to everyone they met.

Far, far away, Wise Men were studying the night sky when they noticed a bright, new glittering star in the east. They discovered that this was a sign that a great king had been born, so they set out to follow the star. They traveled for many days and nights, until finally the star led them to Bethlehem where they found Jesus.

"We have come to see the new king," the Wise Men said, rejoicing that they had found the baby at last. They knelt down to worship Him and presented gifts fit for a king – gold, frankincense, and myrrh.

Everyone was filled with joy at the birth of Jesus.

Away in a Manger

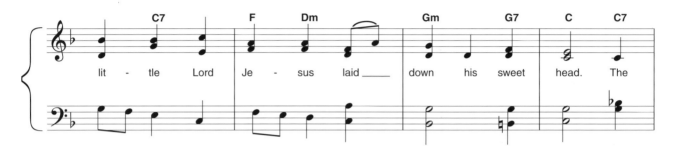

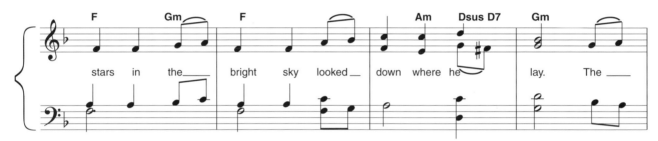

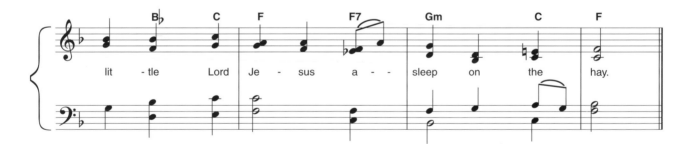

The cattle are lowing, the baby awakes,
But little Lord Jesus, no crying he makes.
I love thee Lord Jesus. Look down from the sky,
And stay by my side until morning is nigh.

How to stage the Nativity

The photographs in this book provide lots of ideas for staging your own nativity play. The costumes are simply made, using one basic pattern for the robes. Find a simple pattern for a loose A-line dress or nightdress. You can adjust the length and sleeves to suit the children involved in the play. Line the edges with bias tape, fastening them at the back. Be adaptable and look for materials in discount stores; consider recycling unwanted items such as old curtains or table-cloths. Raid the Christmas decoration box and find treasures in your sewing basket: old buttons, braid, sequins or sparkly costume jewelery, can all be used to decorate the costumes. Use a craft glue gun to attach decorations.

What you need:

★ MARY
- Long dress with sleeves (from your basic pattern)
- Square shawl – (this can be used later to wrap the baby)
- Dark blue cloak to contrast with dress
- Basket of twigs and small brush

★ JOSEPH
- Long robe (from basic pattern)
- Loose draw-string trousers, or old pair of sweat pants in dark color
- Square of light fabric (i.e. dyed cheesecloth) or tea towel for headdress
- Strip of cord or braided fabric for headband
- Staff for his journey – bamboo with a raffia trim
- Old canvas or raffia travel bag

★ INNKEEPER
- Robe (from basic pattern)
- Apron in contrast fabric (with pocket)
- Large old key on cord to go around neck
- Lantern

★ SHEPHERDS
- Robes in a variety of plain colors in coarse, textured fabric (from basic pattern)
- Contrast color hankerchiefs – bought or made
- Large squares of cheesecloth for headdresses
- Strips of cord or braided fabric for headbands
- Cords with tassels to tie around waists of robes
- Toy lamb (or real one if available)

Shepherds' crooks: Cut a thick stick of bamboo to a suitable length for each child. Wind a double loop of thick, flexible craft wire around the bamboo to secure. Bend the wire into a hooked crook shape. Wind raffia around the crook to disguise the joint between bamboo and wire and secure.

★ WISE MEN
- Robes in rich fabric (from basic pattern)
- Loose, baggy trousers in suitable colors to match/contrast with robes
- Shortened leggings or sweat pants in dark colors.
- Selection of richly patterned scarves, saris, embroidered dressing gowns, colorful fringing, scraps of velvet, and silky fabrics (Use these to wrap around kings as drapes or stoles.)

Headdresses for Wise Men: Take three old baseball caps and remove visors. Wrap pieces of fabric around the caps and secure to create turbans. Wrap more fabric around strips of foam or wadding to create broad padded brims. Secure to headdresses. Add jewels, ribbons, feathers, and decorations.

Gifts for Wise Men: 1. Spray a bottle with paint and add jewels. 2. Paint an old box gold and add jewels for decoration. Fill with gold tinsel and ropes of gold colored beads. 3. Find a suitable container with a lid and decorate. Wrap three boxes using shiny paper.

★ ANGEL GABRIEL

- Long robe with wide sleeves in light-colored silky fabric (from basic pattern)
- Wide strip of contrasting fabric—drape across robe and attach at shoulder and waist with a few stitches
- Decorative braid for neck and sleeves
- Tinsel or stars wound onto hairband for halo
- Large wings *(see separate instructions below)*

★ HOST OF ANGELS

- Sleeveless dresses in a variety of pale, silky fabrics (from basic pattern)
- Tinsel or stars wound onto hairbands for halos
- Wings, sprayed silver or gold *(see instructions)*
- Musical intruments for the angels
- Harp made from cut-out foam board, sprayed gold, with thin silver cord 'strings' and Christmas cherub decorations *(see photo above)*

Angels' wings: Make a pattern using the photo below as a guide. Cut out the shape from one piece of very thin, flexible foam rubber. Attach thick, pliable craft wire to top edge of wings and secure with strong thread. Spray wings on both sides with gold or silver paint. Allow to dry. Glue stars or sequins to top of wings. Attach decorative cord with glue gun or stitch to top edges of wings, covering the wire. Sew cord down the center panel, making a loop at the bottom edge *(see photo below)*. Stretch each piece of cord over opposite shoulders, back through each loop, then together in front. Tie at the waist. The wings should sit quite high on the child's shoulders.

Tweak the wire edge to adjust the wing shape. Make angel Gabriel's wings the same way, but larger.

Cut out feather shapes from gold gift wrap and tissue papers. Stick the feathers in over-lapping rows onto the wings with a glue gun.

Fit the wings onto the child with cords.

★ BACKDROP AND PROPS

Attach silver stars of different sizes to a dark blue curtain or painted backdrop. Add one larger golden star. Recycle old Christmas decorations, buy stars from a party shop, or cut out your own from silver foil.

Arrange several bales of straw or hay on the stage for the children to sit or stand on. Make a manger from a base of bamboo sticks tied together with raffia, or recycle an old box or laundry basket. Fill the manger with hay. Use a life-sized baby doll for the infant Jesus. Wrap the baby in Mary's shawl.